The ABC s of Family Communication

Jean Monbourquette

The ABCs
of
Family Communication

NOVALIS

Translation: Ferdinanda Van Gennip

Cover and Illustrations: Nina Price

Design: Gilles Lépine

© 1994 Novalis, Saint Paul University, Ottawa, Ontario, K1S 1C4

Business Office: Novalis, 49 Front Street East, Second Floor,
Toronto, Ontario, M5E 1B3

Printed in Canada

Canadian Cataloguing in Publication Data

Monbourquette, Jean

   The ABCs of Family Communication

Translation of: L'ABC de la communication familiale

Includes bibliographical references

ISBN 2-89088-709-x

   1. Child rearing. 2. Parent and child.
3. Parenting. 4. Family. I. Title

HQ769.M5813   1995   649'.1   C94-900866-4

NOVALIS

Table of Contents

*This work is dedicated
to all the families who have welcomed me
into the intimacy of their homes.*

Foreword

This is a short handbook on raising children. It is designed for parents who don't have time to read lengthy works on the subject. It was compiled in light of many years of workshops given on parent-child communication and on the basis of information gathered from family therapy sessions. One of the goals of this book is to rekindle in parents the desire to carry out their role with confidence, joy and passion.

This book's text first appeared in manuscript form, guiding countless parents in their role as educators. It also served as a tool for facilitating discussion groups. This edition sports a whole new look after undergoing revision and expansion.

Finally, I would like to thank my friend, Jacques Croteau, O.M.I., for his invaluable assistance in clarifying certain ideas and improving the literary presentation of the text.

Knowing how to acknowledge and appreciate your parental power

Many parents do not feel equal to the task of parenting. They have little confidence in themselves and they are afraid of not being "good parents." They feel overwhelmed by the demands made on them by their family and by society in general. Why do parents feel this way?

There are too many contradictory messages from experts on child-rearing. Some advocate a *laissez-faire* attitude while others favour authoritarian rule. What about the parents' philosophy?

Some schools of thought exaggerate the child's fragility, striking fear in parents' hearts and causing panic with statements like: "A child's character is formed by the age of six."

It is also in vogue to blame parents for all the problems adults experience in their lives. It's easier to make Mum and Dad responsible for one's weaknesses than to take charge of one's life.

There is a tendency for society in general – teachers, politicians and police officers – to burden parents with the full responsibility for the social ills prevalent among young people. These accusations are even stronger when it comes to single-parent families.

In our treatment of this subject we want to help parents reclaim the joy and confidence that should be part and parcel of parenting. We want to assure them that they have within themselves all the resources needed for success. We wish especially to see them recover their parental authority – not an oppressive authority – but one that is founded on their skills and personal competence.

All parents have:

✔ the ability to love;

✔ the ability to organize their family;

✔ the ability to encourage their child to mature;

✔ the ability to listen to their child;

✔ the ability to be affirming;

✔ the ability to negotiate through obstructions;

✔ the ability to influence their child's moral values.

Winning
your child's
co-operation

"**H**ow can I force my child to want to study?" one mother asked me. This question raises the

whole issue of parent-child interaction during the growing-up process.

Parents must remind themselves continually that it is the child who has the primary responsibility for growing up. The child is the primary agent of this process.

How do you go about getting children to be seriously involved in their own development?

Always bear in mind that, while it is instinctive for the child to *want* to grow up, it is the parent's task to guide and encourage the child's efforts to "mature."

So, instead of doing the wanting *for* your child, try to win your child's co-operation by supporting him or her at those times when the desire to develop is expressed.

Developing attitudes favourable to good parenting

As parents, you are not required to be perfect and to know everything right from the start! Learning to raise children is an ongoing process. Realize that you are entitled to make mistakes and to start over. Be patient with yourself as you grow into your parental role.

You and your spouse should try to agree on the general principles you want to follow in raising your child. Avoid competing for your child's affection, especially if you are divorced.

You will achieve more by being calm and relaxed than by worrying and fearing the worst. Obsessive anxiety about your parenting skills may well lead a child to the very behaviour you feared. For instance, an exaggerated fear that your children may get into drugs could well lead them to want to experiment with drugs because of all the attention you have given the topic.

Always remember that children actually grow up themselves. As they get older, learn how to stand back and give them the space they need to exercise their freedom and to mature. Let them do on their own whatever does not require your assistance. In this way they will learn to grow up by themselves. Trying to protect them from the slightest suffering or embarrassment serves to cripple them for life.

Instead of being on the defensive and always needing to say No to your child's requests, why not anticipate them and be prepared to suggest alternative activities? It is much easier to direct a child's energy than to try to block it.

Have the courage to accept not being a perfect parent. Be willing to apologize to your children if you make a mistake. You will be teaching them that they can always start over after making a mistake. Furthermore, every mistake you make offers you a fresh opportunity to learn and grow.

Stop worrying about what your parents, neighbours and friends may think of the way you raise your children. After all, the way you raise your children is *your* responsibility.

Be aware of your desire to find personal fulfillment through the lives of your children – your desire to seek satisfaction in their achievements rather than in their well-being. Remember *who they are* is more important than *what they do*.

If you harbour too much ambition for your children they may become easily discouraged. If a

parent's demands are excessive, children may have difficulty accepting their limitations and failures. Sometimes children are so overwhelmed by their parents' demands that they entertain thoughts of suicide. Other parents, however, lack ambition for their children and tend to "spoil" them. Instead of seeking what is truly good for their child they react to the deprivations of their own youth, saying, for example, "I had nothing when I was growing up, so I'll make sure my kids have everything."

Creating an atmosphere of trust

To win your child's co-operation you need to create an atmosphere of trust. If a relationship of trust exists, your child will be more willing to listen to you and obey you. Here are some things you can do to help establish a trusting relationship with your child:

✔ Be available: If your child wants to talk, whenever possible, stop your work and listen. Spend one-on-one time with your child: go for a drive, run errands together, go fishing, etc.

✔ Be encouraging: Note your child's progress and admire it, no matter how small.

✔ Adapt to your child's height: When communicating with your child bend down to be at the same level or pick your child up so you can see and hear each other better.

✔ Speak your child's language: Use the same tone of voice and the same expressions (even if you need to correct them later).

✔ Enter into your child's world: When your child asks a question, give him or her a chance to explain. Ask, "What would *your* answer be?" When your child is drawing or making up a game, ask, "Would you like to tell me about your picture?" or "Could you show me how to play your game?"

✔ Learn to play and have fun together: Avoid always being serious when you approach your child. It is a good idea, for example, to ask "So, have your grades at school improved?" or "Did you behave well at school today?" Be able to tease each other, to play games and to have fun together.

Helping build your child's self-esteem

In our opinion, the parents' most important task is to help their children build self-esteem. Once self-esteem is established, children are able to take initiatives that will help them to mature and to become increasingly independent.

In their desire to grow, children constantly check with their parents and other significant persons to find out if they are on the right track. The reactions and messages they receive serve as a mirror reflecting a positive or negative image. Thus, it is first of all through the eyes of people who are important to them that children learn to appreciate themselves and to grow up.

We need to distinguish between two kinds of self-esteem: self-esteem for *who one is* and self-esteem for *what one does*. Let's have a look at these two forms of self-esteem and the different messages they can evoke and promote in children.

"I am lovable"

The first form of self-esteem concerns *who one is*. It is manifested through feeling at ease with ourselves – physically, spiritually and emotionally. It also consists of considering ourselves as important and worthy of respect, appreciation and love. It becomes natural for the child to say, "I'm O.K. and I'm lovable."

Some ways of communicating and acting that are likely to evoke this kind of self-esteem in children are as follows. A baby learns self-esteem by being held, washed and fed – in loving ways and accompanied by gentle words and smiles. Later on, children learn just how precious they are in the eyes of their parents through the hugs, the attentiveness in tough times, the willingness to listen and respect a child's feelings and thoughts, and through the signs of love given at the comings and goings from home.

Other ways of being attentive to your child as a person include celebrating birthdays and major transitions such as the beginning of puberty.

It is important, then, to foster this form of self-esteem, to give signs of affection to convey appreciation of the *person* rather than appreciation of an *achievement*. Showing signs of affection in response to a child's performance could cause feelings such as, "I'm only lovable and deserving of affection when I'm obedient and successful," or

"The only time I feel loved is when I get good grades."

"I am capable"

The other form of self-esteem is born out of confidence in one's ability to accomplish certain things and to have some control over one's surroundings. This results in tasks being undertaken and carried out with self-assurance – the child takes the steps needed to succeed and perseveres until the task is completed. What approach will evoke and sustain in children this kind of confidence in their abilities?

Repeated encouragement from parents and other significant persons is necessary. This encouragement should consist of positive remarks, simple observations, congratulations, thank-you's, joyful exclamations and so forth. These expressions will nurture a child's confidence in his or her abilities and the desire to take new risks.

The reward that children value the most for their accomplishments is being noticed by others. This is worth a lot more than presents or money. The words or gestures used to show that their accomplishments are appreciated are gradually interiorized in such a way that it becomes easy for them to visualize being successful.

Recent studies have shown that a child's ability to see a task through to completion depends on this form of self-esteem. It is the quality most lacking among "dropouts," who feel certain of failure before they've even started a job.

The following are a few more suggestions that will help your children develop self-esteem:

✔ Suggest short-term challenges with short-term goals so the chances of success are good. Then, as the taste for success is acquired, suggest more demanding challenges that require greater endurance and perseverance.

✔ Never do for your children what they can do on their own. For instance, if your children ask you for help with a homework assignment, invite them to start independently and to ask for help only when problems arise. And when you *do* help, demand full participation in the search for a solution. Ask questions like: "What happens when . . . ?" or "From what other angle could you approach this?"

✔ Introduce your children to a variety of sports and artistic activities, allowing them to choose what they would like to try. For instance, introduce them to different musical instruments so they can choose which one they would like to play. Once they make a choice encourage them to persevere in it, no matter how frustrated or discouraged they may feel at first. For instance, you might say, "You must continue with your dance classes until the end of the term; at that point we'll sit down together and decide whether you should continue or not."

✔ Explain that a temporary setback, far from being a reason to give up, is often an opportunity to learn and improve.

✔ Have children make choices appropriate for their age. You might ask, for instance, "What would you like to do with the dollar your grandmother gave you today?"

✔ Never pay children to participate in sports or cultural activities, for example, offering two dollars to get them to go to a cub scout meeting.

Avoid things that contribute to low self-esteem

You should not pay your children for doing household chores. You want them to understand they are not employees but rather members of the family. However, payment is recommended for special projects such as agreeing to paint the garage during the holidays. Trusting children to do household chores without being paid develops their sense of responsibility and their sense of belonging to the family.

Weekly allowances should not be considered as salary. An allowance should be seen as the child's share in the family resources – enough to meet his or her needs. For this reason we do not recommend withholding a child's allowance as a punishment.

Children lose their self-confidence when parents try to remove any kind of frustration from their lives or try to prevent them from taking calculated risks. This tends to make children fearful and often irresponsible in the face of life's challenges.

Comparing a child to his or her peers often creates anxiety, a spirit of competition and a sense of powerlessness. It is preferable to measure a child's performance against his or her own previous performance. For instance, you might say, "You made fewer errors on this quiz than on the last one."

Continually drawing attention to a "bad" habit like thumb-sucking only creates anxiety and reinforces the obsession – especially if it is getting your attention and making you angry.

Avoid praising your child for just one quality or just one type of activity. For instance, if you are always repeating, "You should hear how well my daughter plays piano," she may get the idea she is valued only for her piano-playing.

Parents must not become their child's regular leisure-time organizer. Parents may need to organize some of their child's activities, but it is the child who must take the initiative in choosing his or her own friends, games and leisure-time activities.

Using a language of encouragement

Encouragement provides the fuel for a child's self-esteem. When children receive signs of affection and appreciation that are freely given rather than earned, they incorporate them into the ongoing inner dialogue and are able to say, "I am important and lovable." When children receive acknowledgment for performance and are congratulated, they are able to say, "I am a gifted person and I will succeed."

When parent-child communication has broken down, the parents' first strategy for renewing communication should be to start encouraging their child in a consistent and systematic way.

Just as plants need water, so children need encouragement. Without it they become discouraged and behave badly. They become rude, disobedient and destructive, secretly desiring their parents' attention, even if only in the form of reprimands and scoldings, or what psychologists call "negative signs of attention." Punishment feels better than being totally ignored.

How do you let children know you love them for who they are?

There are various ways:

✔ by providing them with what is necessary for their well-being;

✔ by giving them hugs and signs of affection;

✔ by holding them on your lap;

✔ by kissing them hello and good-bye;

✔ by listening to them describe their experience without judging them;

✔ by celebrating their birthdays;

✔ by celebrating special events in their lives such as graduation;

✔ by giving surprise presents once in a while.

Never scold or punish children while giving a sign of affection; they will become thoroughly confused, not knowing what to think. Likewise, never punish children by depriving them of their birthday cake or birthday gift.

Always remember that children should receive hugs and signs of affection not for *what they do* but for *who they are*.

How do you show you appreciate your child's performance?

In order to encourage good behaviour in children show them your appreciation in various ways:

✔ by giving a nod or look of approval, for example, when the garbage is taken out on time;

✔ by reflecting back to them what they experience emotionally: "You seem happy about winning."

✔ by commenting that you have observed their good behaviour: "I notice that you tidied up your clothes."

✔ by offering "I" messages: "I'm so glad to see your room is tidy!"

Watch that you avoid exaggerated and artificial praise ("you're an angel"), judgmental compliments ("you're good when . . .") and humiliating gestures (a pat on the head).

You can discourage negative behaviour by not giving it too much attention.

Try to point out desirable behaviour and to ignore undesirable behaviour.

If a child has become too dependent on your verbal reassurance, sometimes gestures are more effective than words. A smile, a touch or a glance in passing may suffice.

Vary the object of your encouragement according to the different areas in which your child is involved. Avoid always stressing the same area, for instance, musical talent.

You may be able to get your child to obey through humiliating words or gestures, but in the long run this kind of strategy results in low self-esteem and discouragement.

Your child's enjoyment of an activity should be stressed over the results of the project: "You seem to enjoy painting" rather than "My, what a beautiful painting!"

If you have lost your child's confidence, you may have to devote a month or two just to expressing your interest and being encouraging in order to regain that confidence.

Organizing your family environment

A lack of organization and the resulting confusion are a major source of family problems and tensions.

Some parents save themselves a lot of headaches by being a bit creative and turning their home into a multi-learning centre. Here are a few tricks to help you achieve this. Depending on your needs, living quarters can be organized in such a way as to make them:

✔ enriching: educational games, world maps, a shop with practical tools, lists of interesting TV programs, lists of videos, brochures (can be left in the bathroom), a small library, etc.;

✔ peaceful: reducing stimulation will be conducive to sleep at bedtime; for example, closing the curtains in the bedroom, turning down the TV volume, dimming the lights, no more talking after a certain time;

✔ convenient: lowered clothes hooks where the children can hang up their own clothes, small chairs, a "dirty laundry basket" placed within easy reach for everyone;

✔ orderly: toys are kept in the games room, earphones are used with loud music, dangerous products are kept out of children's reach;

✔ open to other areas of activity: walks in the park, museums, playgrounds, interest courses, exchange visits with other adolescents, volunteer work with charitable organizations;

✔ functional: bulletin board, list of jobs to be done, school calendar, sports schedule and other reminders.

Besides organizing the family environment, you need to plan ahead for events involving family members: prepare your child for a visit to the dentist; when travelling bring your child's toys and familiar objects; have your child get acquainted with a new school before attending, etc.

Structuring family life with the help of rules

In single-parent families or in families where both parents work outside the home, top-notch organizational skills are indispensable.

Dialogue among family members will be effective insofar as family life is well structured with respect to schedule, space, rules, job division, etc. For instance, you will not have time each day to discuss meal times or what time to get up.

Rules should be clear and specific. For example, "You may run around in the basement but not in the living room or the kitchen."

Limits should be clearly defined. The following rule is too vague: "It's O.K. to splash your sister with water but don't overdo it."

Respond to your child's behaviour in a way that is consistent with the rule that has been established. When the rule is kept, take note; when it is broken, confront.

Explicit orders are called for in emergency situations. For example, "Get your knife out of the toaster!"

If you must impose a rule, try to offer a choice of behaviours. For example, "Jumping on the living room sofa is not allowed. Do you want to jump on the mattress in the basement or play outside?"

Negative orders such as "Don't touch the vase" reinforce the temptation to do the very thing that is forbidden. It is preferable, therefore, to divert the child's attention to another activity. "Here is your truck" is preferable to "Don't touch my vase." Directing a child's energy is always easier than trying to block it.

Applying "logical consequences" instead of punishment

At first glance rewards and punishments appear to be effective methods of discipline for raising children. However, they are difficult to apply and, in the long run, not very suitable. In fact, as children get older it becomes almost impossible to think of rewards and punishments that are appropriate to their age.

Furthermore, punishments and rewards do not help children develop confidence in their parents. They will quickly learn to use the same pedagogy – behaving in ways that punish or reward their parents.

There are more educational and effective methods for helping children become responsible for their actions. Show them the *natural* and *logical consequences* (a term from Adlerian psychology) of their actions.

Natural consequences are those that result from the nature of the action itself. For instance, a child who believes that a Batman costume will

enable him or her to fly will soon learn the painful truth when jumping off a table to test this belief. Experience is the best teacher.

Logical consequences are those that result from breaking an established rule. For instance, a child who arrives late for supper will find the table cleared and will have to be satisfied with the leftovers from the refrigerator; the kitchen is to be left tidy and clean.

The advantage of logical consequences

Establishing and applying logical consequences is a necessary part of raising children, especially once parents realize that it is not up to them to carry out tasks for which the children themselves are responsible – doing homework, studying for tests, gathering dirty laundry, etc.

Conditions for establishing a logical consequence

A logical consequence must be expressed as a rule of behaviour in the house. The child does not have to agree. It is established by the parent. For example, "If you don't feed your dog, we're going to have to give it away."

It is not a punishment, but it should be applied calmly, strictly, impartially and without any fuss. For example, "When I do the laundry on Monday, I'm only washing the clothes I find in the laundry basket."

When a parent wants to change a rule and create a new logical consequence, here are the steps to follow:

✔ Advise your child you are going to make a change. For example, "Starting tomorrow, I'll only wake you once. After that, without any further warnings from me, you'll be responsible for getting up, having your breakfast and catching the bus. If you miss the bus, you'll have to walk to school."

✔ Stick firmly to your new rule. Be prepared for the likelihood that your child will test your resolve. For instance, he or she may very well get up late and miss the bus. This is precisely when to apply the logical consequence of the negligent behaviour. No note for lateness and no ride to school should be given.

✔ To show that you are firm in applying logical consequences and in order not to give in, you sometimes will need to solicit the support of your spouse or of a friend. (This principle is found in the "tough love" method.)

✔ In applying logical consequences you need to keep words to a minimum and do what you have said – less talk and more action. For instance, "If you're not ready at six, I'm leaving without you."

Examples of logical consequences

Here are some rules to be accompanied by logical consequences. They will make family life much more agreeable.

✔ If you open a jar, close it.

✔ If you unlock a door, lock it.

✔ If you break something, admit it.

✔ If you can't fix something, ask for help.

✔ If you borrow something, return it.

✔ If you make a mess, clean it up.

✔ If you remove something from its place, put it back.

✔ If you want to use something that doesn't belong to you, ask permission.

✔ If you don't know how to operate a piece of equipment, find out before using it.

✔ If it doesn't concern you, don't ask any questions.

✔ If it's not broken, don't try to fix it.

✔ If you drop something, pick it up.

✔ If you take your coat off, hang it up.

✔ If you hear the phone or the doorbell, answer it.

✔ If your pet has a problem, look after it.

✔ If you turn the light on, turn it off.

✔ If you turn the tap on, turn it off.

✔ If someone says hello and smiles at you, return the greeting.

Listening to your child

Active listening means mirroring your child's actions, emotions and intentions. Examples of active listening include:

✔ "You had a good time with your new friend."

✔ "You seem to be angry with your brother."

✔ "I think you want my attention."

✔ "You are happy you did well at school."

Active listening shows children you are interested in how they feel. It helps them to understand themselves better when they feel confused. It improves your relationship with them. It also motivates them to find their own solutions to problems.

Active listening fosters self-esteem in children. It teaches them that having emotions is normal and that emotions become more manageable when they are expressed in a non-destructive manner.

Active listening is neither pity nor approval but simply acknowledging what the child feels at a given moment. To the comment, "My teacher's a real jerk," a listening parent will respond, "Are you angry with him?" In this way you are commenting on the child's emotions and avoiding any judgment on the teacher.

Feeling sorry for a child only increases his or her misery and doesn't resolve anything in the end.

Children also need active listening when they express inner turmoil through either words or behaviour. Think of a child who starts exhibiting unusual behaviour, for instance, by being exceptionally quiet or loud and argumentative.

Active listening is only possible when you have time and do not feel pressured. Postpone it when necessary.

Learn how to read between the lines. The question, "Dad, did you like girls even if they had acne?" is really saying, "I'm self-conscious about my acne and I'm afraid the guys won't be interested in me."

Listening to your child's needs does not oblige you to satisfy them

Every day parents hear hundreds of requests from their children. Therefore they must learn to say No without feeling guilty and without antagonizing their children. Here are some ways you can say No without frustrating your child:

✔ When your child asks you for something, first of all acknowledge his or her need or desire.

✔ Give the reasons why you must refuse the request.

✔ Offer other options that might partially satisfy your child's need or desire. For example, "I know you want to go camping with your friends, but I have to say No because your friends are too old for you and also I don't know them. We're going hiking tomorrow and you're certainly welcome to join us."

Training your child
to be sensitive
to parents' needs

Sometimes a child's behaviour annoys you, disturbs you or gets on your nerves. There are two ways you can intervene to get him or her to stop bothering you. One way is to give a message beginning with the word "you" in the form of a statement, command or threat, for example:

✔ Name-calling: "You're being a real pest, making all that racket when your father is trying to sleep!"

✔ Ordering him or her to stop: "You will stop immediately and go outside."

✔ Making a threat: "If you keep making such a racket you will be sent to your room."

"You" messages are aggressive and label the child as bad, provoking a reaction of either frightened submission or else rebellion.

The other way of intervening is to give a message beginning with the word "I". In this case, the parent is describing an inner reaction to the child's behaviour, for example, "I can't rest when you are making noise in the house."

An "I" message is not aggressive and describes the parent's experience. The child retains a choice about changing his or her behaviour. Pride and self-esteem are left intact as is the affectionate relationship with the parent. A gentle admonition has excellent chances of success without harming the child or damaging the relationship.

While the "I" message is effective in theory, this is not always so in practice – at least at first glance. It may happen that even after a gently given "I" message, a child will react strongly. For instance, to the message, "It frustrates me when you leave your coat lying around because I like a tidy house," a child might easily reply, "You're always nagging me." That is your opportunity to mirror back what you hear: "You think I'm hassling you." Then pick up on your "I" message: "I'm not trying to hassle you. I'm trying to keep the house tidy." From there carry on alternating between "I" messages and active listening. By listening you train the child to listen to you.

Sometimes, after you have given an "I" message in response to unacceptable or disagreeable behaviour, it is good to invite the child to reflect before answering. For instance, "When you call me names, I feel really insulted and very angry; and I would like you to think about the way you are

treating me. We will talk about this tomorrow."
Allowing the child a period of reflection is often
profitable.

(In another chapter we will see that in more
serious situations a parent will need to use confrontation to deal with the situation.)

Understanding why children misbehave

When your child behaves in a strange, rude or rebellious manner and you have the presence of mind and the inner calm needed, ask yourself, "What is my child trying to achieve by behaving this way?" and try to answer by putting yourself in your child's place.

The main goals children unconsciously try to achieve through negative behaviour are the following:

✔ to get your attention when they feel deprived of it;

✔ to be included when their social importance is not sufficiently recognized;

✔ to get revenge when they feel someone has infringed on their rights;

✔ to appear passive, unco-operative, unwilling to satisfy even the smallest request, and to stay isolated, when they want to give you the message that you are a bad parent.

How can you recognize your child's unconscious goals? Take a moment to look at yourself and check what reaction your child's behaviour has provoked in you.

✔ Are you annoyed by this attitude? Are you getting tired of repeating the same instructions over and over? – Your child is probably manifesting a need for attention.

✔ Do you feel you are engaged in a power struggle? – Your child wants to have more power and responsibility.

✔ Do you feel a desire to get even because you were offended? – Your child is seeking revenge for some offense.

✔ Do you feel powerless toward your child? – You may conclude that your child is discouraged and wants to punish you by appearing incompetent and passive.

How should you react in these situations?

Do not act on impulse. That will only make matters worse.

When a child tries to get your attention through bothersome behaviour, ignore him or her. However, when a child tries to do so through appropriate behaviour, pay attention.

Avoid power struggles. Reflect on your own desire to impose your authority at all costs. Learn to share your responsibilities and decisions with your child.

If you sense that your child wants revenge, try to find out how you may have offended him or her. If appropriate, offer an apology or compensation.

Don't let your child's apathy or discouragement discourage you. Be supportive when your child makes even the slightest effort. Take his or her situation seriously and don't get bogged down in self-pity ("Poor me!"). If your child expresses thoughts of suicide or shows suicidal tendencies, take him or her seriously and get help.

Defusing situations of unnecessary confrontation

For there to be confrontation someone has to play the role of adversary. So, when you see that your child wants to confront, attack, or get even with you, don't participate. How do you go about this? By not answering and by withdrawing. In this way you indicate your refusal to enter into the conflict or to support rivalry.

Renew contact and pick up the conversation when things have calmed down.

Do not give in when children use blackmail to get their way. Teach them to make their requests clearly and politely, without beating around the bush.

Don't give toys or candies or anything else to a young child demanding them in a screaming or crying voice; to do so is only to encourage repetition of the behaviour. Wait until the tantrum is over and then decide whether to give your child what he or she wanted.

If you are at your wit's end because of your child's behaviour, give yourself a breather before reacting. Otherwise you risk poisoning the situation and reinforcing hostility between the two of you. By reacting completely contrary to your child's expectations you are able to remove the power he or she had over you.

With babies, remember how short their attention span is and that hiding an object from view is sufficient to make them forget they wanted it.

If your spouse has a conflict with your child try not to interfere. Otherwise, you might alienate your spouse and you would deprive your child of learning to sort out his or her own affairs. If you think your spouse was in the wrong, discuss it in private at a more appropriate time.

If your child confronts you in a very self-assured manner in front of your spouse, check whether there might not be a little conspiracy going on, that is, your child might be acting self-assured because he or she is counting on the other parent's support. A child will be particularly apt to try this approach when things are not going well between the parents. It is important for you and your spouse to keep a harmonious relationship that will allow you to count on each other for support when you need to intervene in your child's behaviour.

Distinguishing between conflicting needs and conflicting values

When there is a parent-child conflict you need to be aware of the nature of the conflict. Is the conflict over material things or over a cultural or moral issue? In the first instance you have a conflict of needs. For example: you argue over TV shows, your daughter monopolizes the phone for hours, your son plays his music so loud you think your eardrums will burst. In the second instance material things are not in question. You very likely have a conflict of moral or cultural values. For example, parents may want their child to appreciate classical music but the child's preference is for rock; parents would like the child to take ballet, but their child wants to work at McDonald's with friends.

In the case of conflicting needs an agreement can be reached by negotiating for a solution that will satisfy both the parent and the child.

In the case of conflicting values it is not as easy to find a solution because, as we shall see below, conflicting values involve more intangibles.

Thomas Gordon points out that all too frequently parents interpret a conflict of values as a conflict of needs. Consequently they launch into unnecessary battles with their adolescents. With respect to certain values, Gordon believes parents should leave their children areas where they have full freedom of choice.

Here are some areas where they might exercise that freedom: how they dress, who their friends are, what career they want, when they want to do homework, how they want their room to look (decorations, photos), minor excesses in personal appearance (jewelry, hair, etc.).

However, when it comes to behaviour that is illegal (taking drugs), immoral by family standards (boyfriend and girlfriend sleeping in the same room) or destructive (dangerous driving), the parent has a right and even a duty to confront the adolescent.

Respecting your child's areas of freedom

Parents need to practise the difficult art of discerning what areas of freedom must be increased and broadened as their children mature.

Letting children make choices

Bearing in mind their level of maturity, place children in situations of having to make choices. Provide them with the opportunity to choose between two toys, two kinds of fruit, even two play activities. On the other hand, do not place them in situations requiring choices that might burden them or be beyond their ability. For example, do not ask them to choose between their parents during divorce proceedings or to choose the colour of the family car.

Letting children enjoy time to themselves and their own space

Children need time to themselves as well as their own space (their room) and their own furniture (desk or work table). They need to have the freedom to be by themselves to work or play alone. Parents should respect their space and their time.

Watch that you don't intrude on their privacy and space too often, for example, with ill-timed, exaggerated hugs or by bursting into their room unannounced or interrupting their games without warning. If children must interrupt their play for meal time, let them know fifteen minutes beforehand.

Giving children an allowance

Giving children a weekly allowance is a good way of teaching them to exercise freedom in the use of money. Know how to adjust the amount according to their needs – those of a child or those of an adolescent. Show that you trust their judgment regarding the use of their money.

Likewise, to develop a sense of responsibility in adolescents, some parents start them on a mini-budget for their own expenses. For instance, "You have twenty-five dollars to buy a pair of pants. It's up to you to find the best deal."

Doing things for your children

Currently many educators consider that parents do too much for their children, thus preventing them from learning to manage for themselves. For example, children count on being driven to all their activities – dances, sports, etc. Why not get

them used to walking, taking the bus or alternatively, asking for a ride with the parent of a friend involved in the same activity?

Judging by the way some parents coddle their children, you would think they feel guilty about not doing enough for them. One educator observed recently on a 50-minute flight that a mother had given her child about forty signs of attention in order to keep the child entertained.

Developing the art of negotiation

In family communication the supreme art to learn is that of negotiating in such a way that everyone comes out a winner.

Negotiation is essential in the case of conflicting needs. When, for example, a child uses a parent's tools or plays the stereo too loud, you have a case of conflicting needs since the child's behaviour has a physical and observable effect on the parent.

In the case of conflicting values there are no physical and observable effects. For example, a child's desire to play the drums conflicts with the parents' desire for their child to play violin; an adolescent's choice of ear-rings conflicts with his or her parents' tastes.

The steps of negotiation for cases of conflicting needs

✔ Prepare the child to accept negotiation. Don't impose it. Choose a private spot and mutually agreeable time and persuade him or her of the value of negotiating for a win/win situation.

✔ The first step in the negotiation consists of determining each party's needs. For instance, the child needs tools to repair a bike; the parents need the tools to be kept in order in their workshop.

✔ Brainstorm to find solutions likely to meet the needs of both parties. This is a creative process and does not involve judging the solutions.

✔ Choose one or two methods or solutions that are most likely to satisfy the needs of both parties.

✔ Come to an agreement on how to implement these solutions. Who will do what? When? Where? How?

✔ Schedule another meeting to evaluate the new solutions and to find out how satisfied each party is. If necessary, re-do the various steps of the negotiation process.

Negotiation teaches children responsibility, problem-solving and conflict management.

Setting up a family council

Family councils give family members a chance to express and develop a sense of their responsibility by participating in decisions that affect the family as a whole.

Family councils should meet every week or two at the same time to discuss both agreeable and disagreeable matters. It is a chance to plan outings and holidays as well as to divide up household chores and to establish certain rules.

Family councils should not be seen by parents as the opportunity to preach or by anyone as the opportunity to gripe. If negative feelings do have to be expressed, avoid going on the offensive with "you" messages but communicate instead through "I" messages such as "When Jason takes too long in the bathroom in the morning, I . . . ."

Deal with only one topic or problem at a time and lead the discussion with questions like: "What can we do about . . . ?"

Those family members who are able can take turns chairing the meeting.

Chairperson's tasks

✔ Begin the meeting on time.

✔ Encourage whoever has the floor to speak freely. Make sure that person has completely finished speaking before you allow someone else to start.

✔ Stay on the same topic until it is exhausted.

✔ Speak at the end after all family members have expressed themselves.

Rules for family meetings

✔ The person who has the floor may speak as long as he or she wishes.

✔ Attendance is optional.

✔ No decision should be taken concerning an absent member.

✔ All decisions are subject to revision.

✔ To call or cancel a meeting the approval of all family members is required.

✔ Proceed by consensus rather than by vote.

✔ If it seems useful, have family members make a contractual commitment to carry out certain household tasks or to follow through on a resolution.

Influencing your child's search for values

There is a happy medium between imposing moral values and giving up on the job of moral upbringing: guiding children in their choice of values, a choice only *they* can make. How do you influence their choice of values?

The example of parents and significant others

Example remains the greatest determining factor in moral development. Responsibility teaches responsibility, honesty teaches honesty, patience teaches patience.

Children pay more attention to parents' concrete actions than to their moralizing speeches. When parents' behaviour contradicts their moral discourse children usually tend to imitate their parents' behaviour. For example, if a father tells his sons they should respect girls but is seen viewing pornographic films, his words will have little positive influence.

Asking a child to have morals the parent does not have leads to confusion; for example, an alcoholic father telling his daughter not to take drugs.

This applies to teaching religious values as well. A life of faith on the part of the parent – such as prayer and committed religious practice – will have more impact on the child than the most eloquent sermons on religion.

In order for the parents' moral example to be effective they must ensure the quality and balance of their own moral lives. For instance, they need to avoid extremes. Any virtue taken to its extreme will lead children to develop the opposite fault:

indulgent parent	–	undisciplined child
meticulously responsible parent	–	irresponsible child
overly demanding parent	–	lazy child
controlled parent	–	excitable child.

Since moral progress is an ongoing thing, parents constantly need to be reconciling the various dimensions of their moral life, thus setting for their children an example of moral balance that is as balanced and appealing as possible.

Parents who acknowledge their mistakes and make an effort to correct them are, by their honesty and humility, teaching their children an invaluable lesson.

Parents may rightly ask a child not to begin a bad habit that they themselves have, as long as they honestly admit the difficulty they have experienced in trying to break it. A father might say to his son, "I sure hope you'll never become a smoking addict like me."

Offer explanations for moral values and behaviours

You need to have plenty of solid arguments that will demonstrate the basis for certain moral and religious practices (testimony, statistics, historical facts and reports from experts). Choose an appropriate moment to make a convincing presentation on the importance of certain moral values or behaviours and the basis for them, for example, "The statistics on adolescent marriage show that...." We recommend that parents not go beyond *presenting* the information. If you are too emphatic or repetitious you may be disposing the child to reject your viewpoint ("Yeah, yeah, I know...").

Finally, if you present your convictions in an authoritarian or aggressive way you might detract from the impact of the content itself and alienate your child or adolescent.

Let them make up their own minds

After discussing with children or adolescents the various aspects and consequences of a given moral conduct, show that you have confidence in them that, when they are placed in the same circumstances, they will be able to make the right decision for themselves.

To deal with children in this way, once they have reached an appropriate level of maturity, is the most beautiful way for parents to show openness, respect and generosity toward them. When it comes to the moral development of children and adolescents, all that parents really can do is accompany and assist them in developing their moral judgment, their powers of discernment, and their ability to integrate the values learned at home with those promoted by society.

Other considerations

Before condemning "young people," show you are willing to be challenged by them. For example, give more casual, up-to-date clothing a try, or get involved in the ecology movement.

Nonetheless, adolescents expect parents to live in keeping with their convictions, even though they, the adolescents, may not hold the same convictions. For example, an adolescent who was not attending Mass challenged his father to convince him of the benefits of attending. The father didn't know what to say and – to his son's great disappointment – stopped going to church on Sundays.

Avoid discussions on morality or religion that turn into power struggles.

It might be a consolation for parents to know that children adopt 90% of the moral convictions learned from their family.

Deciding when to intervene when children argue

When children get into an argument avoid being the judge or referee. By giving attention to their conflict you encourage them to keep on arguing or to start up again. The best strategy is to withdraw when the argument erupts. Let them settle their own differences; then they will be less likely to provoke each other in the future.

Don't automatically trust the younger or weaker party. He or she will often try to take advantage of the situation to win your sympathy and get the older or stronger party punished.

When they fight, separate children and treat them the same. For example, send them to their room and take away whatever they were fighting over.

Teach them ways of resolving their differences peacefully. For example, flip a coin to see who will get to use a certain area or object and for how long. Use the stove or micro-wave timer to signal the start of the other person's turn.

Confronting your child about destructive behaviour

What is confrontation?

The kind of confrontation we are talking about consists of advising the child respectfully but firmly that he or she is to end the illegal, immoral or destructive behaviour in which he or she is engaged.

To correct this type of behaviour negotiating would be out of the question. The naive social worker who convinced a single mother to negotiate with her son how often he would be allowed to smoke marijuana in the house is not to be emulated.

Parents are not the cause of their child's delinquent behaviour but they are forcibly implicated. At some point they must intervene. Sooner or later all parents find themselves in the situation of having to confront their child. Unfortunately a great many parents shy away from this responsibility out of fear or lack of courage. What they should know is that a well-handled confrontation is likely to change the course of a child's life for the better and spare him or her a lot of problems in the long run.

Here is a sampling of the kinds of behaviour that call for confrontation:

✔ Your son is accumulating valuable items in his room and you cannot help wondering how he obtained them.

✔ Your fourteen-year-old daughter was drunk at a wild party.

✔ Your eight-year-old is torturing frogs.

✔ Your eighteen-year-old was racing your car along a busy highway.

✔ You find marijuana in your son's room.

✔ You find contraceptives in your thirteen-year-old daughter's purse.

✔ Your daughter is part of a gang that vandalizes property after they've been drinking.

✔ Your son is playing games that can lead to suicide, for example, *Dungeons and Dragons*.

Conditions for successful confrontation

✔ The confrontation must be based on fact.

✔ Confront your child at the first opportunity once you have obtained specific information on the dangerous behaviour. Don't bury your head in the sand.

✔ Confront only when you are able to be calm and objective.

✔ Ignore false excuses and demand real explanations.

✔ Make it clear that your child will have to bear all the consequences of his or her actions and that you are not going to "take the rap."

✔ Do not give a punishment but indicate that you will apply the logical consequences of the action. For example, "If you are not willing to explain why you have a pound of marijuana in your room, I will have to call the police."

✔ Arm yourself with perseverance and patience and seek the support of your spouse or your friends. You will need it in order to hold on throughout the course of a confrontation that may drag on over several days or even several weeks.

The dynamics of confrontation

During a confrontation your role is to be a facilitator – helping your child get out of the "mess" he or she has gotten into. To that end you should follow these steps:

✔ Ask your child to explain his or her illegal, immoral or destructive behaviour. For example, the child is preparing for exams using stolen exam papers.

✔ Once your child has explained the situation to you satisfactorily, ask what consequences he or she expects will result from the unacceptable behaviour.

✔ Once your child has realized the harmful consequences of the behaviour in question, ask how he or she plans to get out of the situation that has resulted.

✔ Help your child to establish a plan of action to correct his or her behaviour and to make restitution for any harm.

✔ Watch that you do not become too involved in each of these steps, lest you end up taking over the role of the child or adolescent. For it is the latter's responsibility to become aware of the destructive nature of his or her behaviour, to assess the consequences and to draw up an action plan to rectify the situation.

Encouraging your adolescent's desire for freedom

Many parents are apprehensive about the onset of their child's adolescent years. They have heard that this is a difficult period and they have built up exaggerated fears. Some of them, having had an unhappy adolescence or having been deprived of the adolescent experience, are so anxious about the problems of that age that they unconsciously provoke them. All these fears and apprehensions do nothing to help create a healthy atmosphere in which adolescents can grow. Parents need not cross that bridge until they come to it.

Studies on adolescence have shown that all physiological and psychological developments at that age are preparing adolescents to leave home, even though their immediate circumstances make that impossible. This contradiction makes them feel torn between wanting to stay at home and wanting to leave home; it is also the reason they feel both very close to their family and yet hemmed in by family rules. It explains the tendency to take advantage of family benefits while wanting desper-

ately to belong to a gang; it explains why the opinions of peers have more weight than parental advice; and it explains why they desire experiences of their budding sexuality and of the altered states that drugs can produce.

Parents, then, are a bit like air traffic controllers in an airport tower. They witness the performance of young pilots, flying for the first time while still depending on an instructor. Then, one day, they witness the solo flight. From their vantage point, parents still maintain constant communication with their apprentice pilot. They still control the duration of the flight and the itinerary so that they can direct the pilot to a safe landing at the right time.

Adolescents need to have some experience of leaving home without leaving for good. Consequently, it is recommended that teenagers be allowed to have "sleep-overs" at their friends' homes when the parents know the family. It satisfies their need to get away while still maintaining close family ties.

During these outings adolescents have the opportunity to experience their freedom and to learn how to establish new relationships. It is an opportunity to test the skills learned at home, especially those of self-esteem and autonomy.

Helping your child through bereavement

One of life's most important lessons is learning how to say good-bye to a loved one who has died. Parents must therefore familiarize their children with death and teach them how to deal with grief positively.

Often the death of a small animal will provide parents with an ideal opportunity to answer the questions children have about death and to hear the explanations children themselves have of death. If it seems appropriate a burial ritual could be held for the animal. It helps children prepare for saying good-bye to persons they love.

You need not be afraid to bring children to the funeral home if they want to come. On the other hand you must never force them to attend. It is good to prepare them beforehand for what they will find. Explain for example, "Grandma will look like she is sleeping in a casket; she will not move or talk but you may touch her; her body will be cold and unresponsive but she will still know you are nearby."

Keep children's visits to the funeral home short and don't leave them alone while you are there, unless other people can look after them. During the funeral service you might invite a child to draw a picture of the deceased person or to recall the happy moments spent with that person.

During their bereavement children cannot stand to be sad for very long. Their grief is not continual, as an adult's is. They can switch suddenly from sadness to joy if they feel like playing or having fun. On the other hand sometimes weeks after the death, when no-one is expecting it, a child shows sorrow on remembering the deceased person.

Children have difficulty grasping the irreversible nature of death. Consequently they will sometimes ask when the deceased person is coming back.

Occasionally children will feel guilty about the death of a parent or someone close to them, blaming themselves for having caused a lot of trouble or for being difficult. When this happens you need to help children express their feelings and then reassure them that they are in no way responsible for the death of the person.

Children learn bereavement by imitating family members. The more that death and bereavement appear to be natural events in a family, the easier it will be for children to live through them and integrate them into their lives. They will thus be better prepared to deal with other losses they will have to face.

Protecting your child during marriage breakdown

It cannot be denied that during marriage break-down, children are seriously hurt. As a result of the family breaking up, children experience serious trauma, but parents can mitigate and reduce it by their words and attitudes.

✔ Reassure the child several times that even if Mum and Dad are separating, they will keep on loving and taking care of their child.

✔ Remind your child continually that he or she was created in love and by love and that Mum and Dad will always appreciate the beauty of their creative act and will never have any regrets about it.

✔ Convey as clearly as possible the reasons for the separation, without elaborating too much on the details.

✔ Reassure the child often that he or she is in no way responsible for the separation and that it is a matter between Mum and Dad.

✔ Anticipate that the child might sometimes react aggressively and take it out on one parent or the other, unjustly accusing him or her of having caused the separation.

The feelings of aggression in boys may manifest themselves in delinquent behaviour at home or at school, while in girls it is more likely to take the form of isolation and withdrawal. Encourage children to express their feelings verbally rather than by causing harm.

Just as children somehow tend to imagine that their parents' separation is their fault, they may also believe it is their mission to re-unite their parents. Some will even go so far as to get into trouble in order to force their parents to get back together to deal with the problem.

The greatest desire of children of broken homes is to see their parents talk to each other.

If possible encourage children to join groups of others who are going through the same thing so they can share their feelings about the whole experience.

Living in a single-parent family

In certain cases it can be very painful for children to choose with which parent they would prefer to live, for fear that by choosing one parent they will lose the affection of the other. In the case of young children, it is better for the parents to decide. In the case of adolescents, it is better that they themselves make the decision.

When you need to talk about the absent parent in the presence of a child, watch that you don't destroy the image of that parent in the child's eyes. Nor should you idealize the other parent, for the child will rightly wonder why you and your spouse divorced.

If the child wants to know the reason for the separation, present the facts as objectively as possible. For example, "Your father was involved with another person and I could not tolerate that kind of situation."

Avoid using your child as a source of information about the life of your ex-spouse. A child feels

very uncomfortable in the role of informant. It is always better to address your ex-spouse directly. Parents must settle the question of covering children's living expenses. If children wish to have a special allowance they themselves will have to be able to negotiate that with their parents.

The parent who has custody is vulnerable to being blackmailed, since children will sometimes threaten to go and live with the other parent if they don't get what they want. You must try to ignore these attempts at manipulation. By the same token, children must not be threatened with being sent to the other parent when *you* are angry.

Be faithful and punctual for your visits with your child. Children easily feel rejected if you do not show up or if you arrive late.

Create an area that will be your child's own space when he or she comes to visit you. Clear some space and empty some drawers for your child's personal belongings.

There are two dangers that threaten the parent-child relationship in a single-parent family. The first is that of substitution. The child may try to replace the absent spouse and this will seriously complicate the psychological development of the child, whether a boy or a girl. The second danger is that the parent living with the child will see in him or her unfavourable character traits of the ex-spouse and begin to feel antipathy toward the child as a result. It is not uncommon to hear a parent say, "You're making me angry just the way your father always did."

If an adolescent boy starts becoming violent toward his mother, ask his father to take him because this is often a sign that he needs a masculine presence. If the father has disappeared or refuses to take his son, the mother needs to find a male friend who can take her son in and look after him.

Helping your child adapt to a "blended" family

Before thinking of starting a new life with another companion, parents should leave enough time to ensure they have said farewell to the relationship that has just ended. This will also allow children the time they need to mourn the loss of their family's wholeness.

Divorced parents who start dating should protect the privacy of the home and spare the child from having to meet various partners. When they are sure of the seriousness of the relationship, they should first talk to the child about it, being very attentive to his or her reactions to the arrival of a new person in the family. If the parent and child have lived alone together for a long time, some jealousy may be expected. The child might view the stranger's arrival as a violation of the intimacy that he or she has developed with the parent.

In most "blended" families the source of the problem is not the adults who love each other, but the children who feel forced to accept someone – whom they did not choose – into their lives. Often the parent is so enthralled by the new relationship that he or she expects it to be instantaneously accepted by the child. Children will react all the more strongly if they have not yet given up their dream of seeing their parents reunited. They will simply consider the parent's new friend or lover as an intruder.

What often adds to the young person's confusion and irritability is that the new friend takes on the mission of playing super Mum or super Dad. No matter how much attention the new person showers on the child, the latter will feel obliged to remain faithful to the absent parent. So it is important to respect the child's rhythm of getting acquainted and comfortable with the new spouse and coming round to accepting the latter as a friend.

The newcomer must not try to discipline the child in a parental manner. This should only be authorized through delegation if the natural parent is absent, just as would happen with a baby-sitter.

When both the parents of a blended family have children, they should expect conflicts to arise between their respective children at some point. This will challenge them to demonstrate fairness in the treatment of their own children as well as their spouse's children.

"Your children
are not
your children"

As I complete this work I am aware I have "bombarded" you with a lot of advice, perhaps giving you the impression that only *you* are responsible for raising your children. Perhaps I lost sight of the counsel I gave at the beginning: children must raise themselves.

Indeed, parents – you who have invested so much love and energy in bringing up your children – will be asked to set them free to make the journey of Life. Consider, however, that you have done your duty if you have awoken in them the inner Voice that will accompany and lead them throughout their lives.

In conclusion I would like to leave you with this reflection by Kahlil Gibran:

Your children are not your children

They are the sons and daughter's
of Life's longing for itself.
They come through you
but not from you,
And though they are with you
yet they belong not to you.
You may give them your love
but not your thoughts,
For they have their own thoughts.
You may house their bodies
but not their souls,
For their souls dwell in the house of tomorrow,
which you cannot visit, not even in your dreams.
You may strive to be like them,
but seek not to make them like you.
For life goes not backward
nor tarries with yesterday.

Recommended Reading

General works on the family

Bock, Lois and Miji Working. *Happiness is a Family Time Together*. New Jersey: Fleming H. Revell Company, 1975.

Bessel, Harold and Thomas Kelley. *The Parent Book: The Holistic Program for Raising the Emotionally Mature Child*. San Diego, California: Psych/Graphic Publishers, 1977.

Encouragement and logical consequences

Dreikurs, Rudolf. *Children: The Challenge*. New York: Duell, Sloan and Pearce, 1964.

Zuckerman, Lawrence and others. *A Parents' Guide to Children: The Challenge*. New York: Hawthorn Books Inc., 1978.

Communication

Gordon, Thomas. *Parents Effectiveness Training: The No-Lose Program for Raising Responsible Chidlren*. New York: P. H. Wyden Books, 1970.

Gordon, Thomas. *Parents Effectiveness Training in Action*. New York: P. H. Wyden Books, 1976.

Self-esteem

Briggs, Dorothy. *Your Child's Self-Esteem: The Key to His Life.* New York: Doubleday, 1975.

Sinclair, Donna and Yvonne Stuart. *Christian Parenting.* Winfield, BC: Wood Lake Books Inc., 1990.

Confrontation

Marshall, Bill and Christina Marshall. *Better Parents, Better Children: A Workbook for a More Successful Family in 21 Days.* New Jersey: Hammond, 1979.

York, Phyllis and David. *Toughlove.* Garden City, New York: Doubleday, 1982.

Disciplining children

Ginott, Haim. *Between Parent and Child: New Solutions to Old Problems.* New York: Avon, 1968.

Disciplining adolescents

Ginott, Haim. *Between Parent and Teenager.* New York: Macmillan, 1969.

McCoy, Kathy. *Coping with Teenage Depression: A Parent's Guide.* New York: Simon and Schuster, 1981.

Children and divorce

Gardner, Richard. *The Boys' and Girls' Book about Divorce: With an Introduction for Parents.* New York: J. Aronson, 1983.

Stollman, Wilma. *Stepfamilies: Making Yours a Success.* (1985). Family Services – Canada, 220 Laurier West, Ottawa, ON K1P 5Z9. Tel.: (613) 230-9960.